PURE BREAKOUT
FOR STOCK MARKET

GOPAL SAINI

ISBN 978-1-68538-721-1

Contents

Contents

Disclaimer

Unique experience and past performances do not guarantee future results. Trading stocks, commodities, index, future, options and Forex currencies involves substantial risk and there is always the potential for loss. Your trading results may vary.

No representation is being made that any software or training will guarantee profits.

All trading operations involve serious risks, and you can lose your entire investment. No trades are recommendations or advice and we cannot be sued for losses of capital and Author is not liable for any loss of capital. All trading strategies are for educational purposes only. Contact your financial adviser for trading.

CHAPTER ONE

What is a Breakout?

A breakout means when the price of a stock, commodity, currency etc. moves above a resistance area or moves below a support area. The breakout indicate the possibility for the price to start trending in the breakout direction. In other words we can say that the direction is change now.

For example the price break the resistance level and close above the resistance level with higher volume (relative to normal volume) show greater conviction which means the price is more likely to go up trend in the breakout direction.

And other side the price break the support level and close below the support level with higher volume (relative to normal volume) show greater conviction which means the price is more likely to go down in the breakout direction.

CHAPTER TWO

Features of a Valid Breakout

If you trade in breakout strategy you have to remember these points in your mind. Because breakouts can be subjective since not all traders will recognize or use the same support and resistance levels.

1. Breakouts provides more wining trading opportunities in any segment of the market.
2. A valid breakout is when the price of a stock, commodity, currency etc. moves above a resistance level or moves below a support level.
3. A breakout to the upside of resistance level indicates that a trader should either buy or square off sell positions. A breakout to the downside of support level indicates that a trader should sell or square off buy positions.
4. Breakout must or may be with high volume therefore the price is more likely to continue moving in the breakout direction.
5. Breakouts on low relative volume are more prone to failure. So the price is less likely to trend in the breakout direction.

CHAPTER THREE

Examples of Breakout

In the financial market, chart patterns are very important especially Japanese candle stick chart pattern, most of the traders are using this pattern that should be utilised as part of your technical analysis strategy from beginners to professionals.

Trading chart patterns often from shapes, which can help predetermine price action, such as breakout patterns and reversals patterns. Recognising chart patterns will help you gain a competitive advantage in the market and using them will increase the value of your future technical analyses. Before starting your chart patter analysis, it is important to familiarise yourself with the different types of chart breakouts.

1. Ascending triangle
2. Descending triangle
3. Symmetrical triangle
4. Pennant
5. Flag
6. Wedge
7. Double top
8. Double bottom
9. Head and shoulders
10. Cup and handle
11. Rounding bottom etc.

In the financial market lots of trading patterns are there and from beginners to professionals are using them, and some of traders are develop their own patterns.

Charts patterns can sometime be quite difficult to identify on trading charts when you are beginner and even when you are professional trader.

In the next topic I will explain you which chart pattern breakout is more powerful and how to identify on chart in easy manner.

After doing some practice you will also able to identify and draw these pattern easily.

CHAPTER FOUR

Which Breakout is Powerful?

As you know that there are lots of breakout chart patterns in the financial market. But from my last 10 years' experience of trading I observe that only some patterns are more important which are given below:

1. Higher high – Lower higher breakout

    Or
    Lower higher – Lower high breakout
    (For long/buying trade).

2. Lower low – higher low breakout

    Or
    Higher low – Higher low breakout
    (For short/selling trade)

3. Range breakout
4. Support and resistance breakout
5. Trend breakout

In the coming topics I will explain these pattern one by one. And before live trading, first you will do practice of these patterns on chart and when you will become perfect and comfortable then go for live trade.

CHAPTER FIVE

Higher High & Lower High Or Lower High & Lower High Breakout

(Only for Long / Buying Trade)

This breakout pattern is most effective and powerful for Intraday, swing and positional trade and easy to identify on chart.

Time frame:

15 minutes for Intraday

1 hr. or more for swing and positional

Method to Identify on chart:

1. First we will see two points HH & LH or LH & LH.
2. Now we will join these two points with trend line.
3. Now wait for a bullish candle close to above the trend line.
4. High and Low of the bullish candle must be above the trend line.
5. If this criteria is met, we will buy on next candle.

Target:

1% to 3% for intraday

5% to 15% for swing and positional

Stop loss:

If a Bearish candle close below the trend line we will exit from the long trade and high and low of bearish candle must be below the trend line.

CHAPTER SIX

Lower Low & Higher low Or Higher Low & Higher Low Breakout

(Only for Short / Selling Trade)

This breakout pattern is most effective and powerful for Intraday, swing and positional trade and easy to identify on chart.

Time frame:

15 minutes for Intraday

1 hr. or more for swing and positional

Method to Identify on chart:

1. First we will see two points LL & HL or HL & HL.
2. Now we will join these two points with trend line.
3. Now wait for a bearish candle to close below the trend line.
4. High and Low of the bearish candle must be below the trend line.
5. If this criteria is met, we will sell on next candle.

Target:

1% to 3% for intraday

5% to 15% for swing and positional

Stop loss:

If a Bullish candle close above the trend line we will exit from the short trade and high & low of bullish candle must be above the trend line.

CHAPTER SEVEN

Range Breakout

A Range Breakout means market is laying in a small price range or movement, of last 15 to 20 candle of any time frame. If the range breaks in any direction, there is a big chance that the price action will continue in the same direction.

Time frame:

15 minutes for Intraday

1 hr. or more for swing and positional

Method to Identify on chart:

1. Check whether the price of a stock or commodity is in a range.
2. Range should be less with small candles.
3. Number of candles should not be more than 15 to 20.
4. Consider the volume of the candle that will break the range, the volume should be higher in comparison with last 15 to 20 candles.

When to Buy:

When a candle break the upper range with higher volume and also close above the upper range then buy on the next candle.

Target:

1:1 or 1:2 or 1:3 of the Range Size

Stop Loss:

50% of Range Size

When to Sell:

When a candle break the lower range with higher volume and also close below the lower range then sell on the next candle.

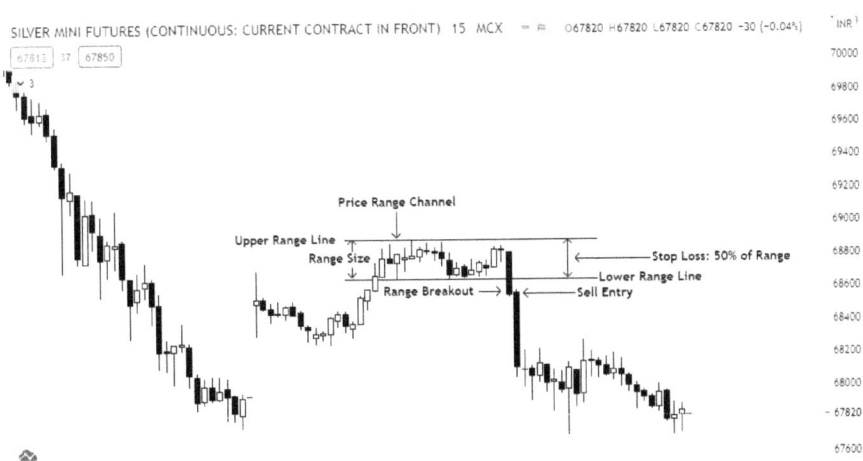

Target:
1:1 or 1:2 or 1:3 of the Range Size
Stop Loss:
50% of Range Size

CHAPTER EIGHT

Support & Resistance Breakout

First we should know that what a support level and resistance level is.

What is a support?

The support level represents a price of a stock or commodity, where the price struggles to fall below over a given time period.

Support levels can be visualized by using different technical indicators or simply by drawing a line connecting the lowest lows for the period.

We can apply trend lines or moving averages to find out more dynamic view of support level.

In other words we can say price of a stock or commodity struggles to fall below a particular price and bounce back after touching that price, if this occur more than 2 or 3 times then it's called support level.

What is a Resistance?

The Resistance level represents a price of a stock or commodity, where the price struggles to rise above over a given time period.

Resistance levels can be visualized by using different technical indicators or simply by drawing a line connecting the highest high for the period.

We can apply trend lines or moving averages to find out more dynamic view of resistance level.

In other words we can say the price of a stock or commodity struggles to rise above a particular price and bounce back after touching that price, if this occur more than 2 or 3 times then it's called resistance level.

Now we will see how to apply and how to use support and resistance breakout for trade.

Time frame:

15 minutes for Intraday

1 hr. or more for swing and positional

Target:

1% to 3% for intraday

5% to 15% for swing and positional

Method to Identify on chart

Buying setup by using Resistance Level breakout

1. Draw a horizontal line where a stock or commodity create a resistance level and bounce back 2 or 3 time over a particular time frame.
2. When a candle break the resistance level with higher volume and also close above the resistance level then buy on the next candle.
3. Consider the volume of the candle that will break the resistance line, the volume should be higher in comparison with last 15 to 20 candles.

Stop Loss: If a Candle close below the resistance line, we will exit form such buying trade.

Sell setup by using Support Level breakout

1. Draw a horizontal line where a stock or commodity create a Support level and bounce back 2 or 3 time over a particular time frame.
2. When a candle break the support level with higher volume and also close below the support level then sell on the next candle.

3. Consider the volume of the candle that will break the support line and the volume should be higher in comparison with last 15 to 20 candles.

Stop Loss: If a Candle close above the support line, we will exit form such sell trade.

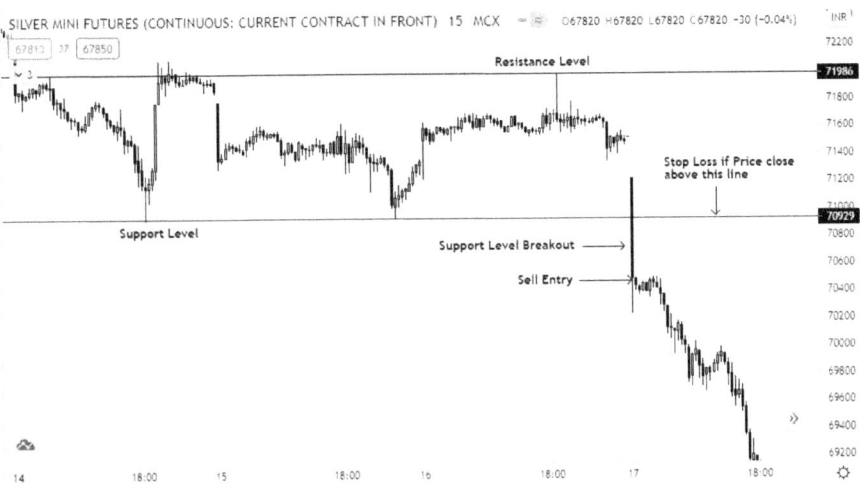

CHAPTER NINE

Trend Breakout

The three basic types of trends are uptrend, downtrend and sideways market.

What is an Uptrend?

An uptrend refers to the price of a stock or commodity, when the overall direction is upward. In an uptrend, each successive high is higher than the previous high.

Example of uptrend

What is a Downtrend?

A downtrend refers to the price of a stock or commodity, when the overall direction is downward. In a downtrend, each successive low is lesser than the previous low.

Example of downtrend

What is a Sideways Trend?

A Sideways trend is the horizontal price movement in a particular range that occurs of supply and demand are nearly equal.

This typically occurs during a period of consolidation before the price continues a prior trend or reverse into a new trend.

Example of Sideways Trend

Now, you understood about the market trend, and we will try to find out when these above trends reverse and will get buy or sell opportunity buy using trend breakout pattern.

When to BUY if market is in Down Trend or
How to find trend reversal or
Down Trend Breakout
Time frame:
15 minutes for Intraday
1 hr. or more for swing and positional
Target:
1% to 3% for intraday
5% to 15% for swing and positional
Points to remember when you buy a stock or commodity in trend breakout strategy:

1. Market should be in the down trend, making a higher low and lower high.
2. We will mark each lower high with a horizontal line.
3. When market price close above the last lower high, we will buy on the next candle.

Stop Loss: If candle close below the horizontal line, we will exit from such buy trade.

Points to remember when you sell a stock or commodity in trend breakout strategy:

1. Market should be in the uptrend, making a lower high and higher low.
2. We will mark each higher low with a horizontal line.
3. When market price close below the last higher low, we will sell on the next candle.

Stop Loss: If candle close above the horizontal line, we will exist from such sell trade.

CHAPTER TEN

How to use valid Breakout For Intraday Trading

Every breakout strategy which is given in the previous topics, can also be used for intraday trading with more efficiency and accuracy.

First you have to see higher time frame chart of same strategy.

For example if you are using HH-LH or LH-LH breakout strategy for buying in any stock or commodity. Then, first you have to draw this strategy in Daily time frame.

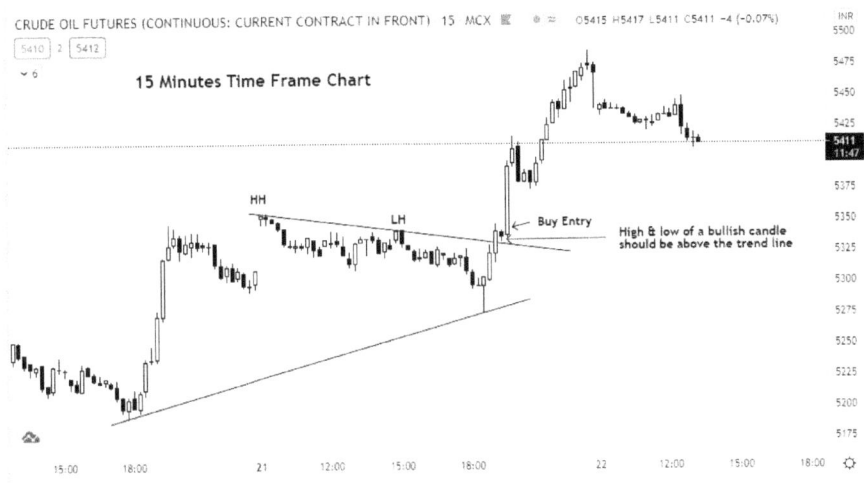

CRUDE OIL FUTURES (CONTINUOUS: CURRENT CONTRACT IN FRONT) 15 MCX ⬚ ✦ ≈ O5415 H5417 L5411 C5411 −4 (−0.07%)

15 Minutes Time Frame Chart

Buy Entry

High & low of a bullish candle should be above the trend line

HH
LH

Although all above given breakout patterns are very useful for trading in any segment and duration like Intraday trading or swing trading or positional trading, but

Higher High – lower Higher and

Lower Low – Higher Low is more effective.

So, first do more and more practice before live trading. when you become perfect and comfortable with confidence then go for live trading.

My best wishes with you

HAPPY TRADING JOURNEY

www.ingramcontent.com/pod-product-compliance
Lightning Source LLC
Chambersburg PA
CBHW070847220526
45466CB00002B/909